I0192006

All Of The Life In My Little Black Body

I was six or seven, maybe, and I was in my backyard playing when a few, kids a few years older than me, rolled up and surrounded me. I had no clue what they wanted and I didn't care and I wasn't scared because that's a learned behavior. The leader punched me in the temple and asked me to give him my pants and I refused. I yelled for my brother because I couldn't win the fight alone and they ran. My mom chased them through the neighborhood in a caravan.

Wee-Bey made love and Namond Brice came out of it, I'm showing my conditioning by mentioning that I'm disappointed that Namond never stood tall.

Kain spent everyday with O Dogg and survived Harold slipping at the light and a bullet wound but when he died it was over a girl he had sex with once.

Bobby Johnson scratched his tears off and came home and his son was disgusted.

Ricky was probably faster than me.

This pigmentation, my noticeably high concentration of melanin, means more than anything that my story won't always make sense...the pieces won't always fit together nicely. However, strung throughout are inescapable truths and those truths and their implications make it all worth it.

Black dissonance is the gift because it manages to still make good music and lovely stories; it's also the curse and so far our only inheritance.

All Of The Life In My Little Black Body

Austin Vandorian Grier

Red Tint Tours

2015

Copyright © 2015 by Austin Vandorian Grier

All rights reserved. This book or any portion thereof may not be reproduced or used in any manner whatsoever without the express written permission of the publisher except for the use of brief quotations in a book review or scholarly journal.

Front Cover Painting: "The Apotheosis Of Illness" by Austin Vandorian Grier

Back Cover Painting: "Kingdom Come at Igbo Landing" by Austin Vandorian Grier

First Printing: 2015

ISBN: 978-0-578-16571-4

Red Tint Tours
3206 Forestview Dr
High Point, North Carolina 27260

www.TheRedTint.com

Ordering Information:

Special discounts are available on quantity purchases by corporations, associations, educators, and others. For details, contact the publisher at the above listed address.

U.S. trade bookstores and wholesalers: Please contact Red Tint Tours Tel: (336) 307-8121 or email Grier.Austin@gmail.com

Dedication

to those who would die of thirst on an island in the middle of a freshwater lake while staring at a clear blue sky with mouth wide open waiting for rain

and to those who know salvation when they see it

Contents

Acknowledgements

I would like to thank all the people I have ever met and

Professor Yogi for the prayers and the books
Deacon Grier for teaching me to be a man
Ju for everything
Trizzy for riding through the city with me
Shevy for your words and refuge
Mrs. Little for seeing a laureate
King Vaya for your expertise

Preface

I want to give you something worthy of your genius; I do not want your love, only your time and attention...I want your sober deliberation.

I want to give you something worthy of your faculties; only our greatest creation will suffice. Man's greatest invention is the anecdote. We were taught early on that there could be no plot without a problem. I wrote this book because they left out the man and the quote that told us that the problem of the twentieth century was that of the color line.

I want to tell you a story worthy of your reflection. I want to paint for you a plot and a problem. I want to tell you what it is to be black and little and American and studied and ridiculed and copied and murdered and celebrated.

I want to demonstrate love and plight for you so you'll know my story and your own.

AV

Austin Vandorian Grier

Prologue – The Freed Fruit Manifesto

I wrote a book when I was younger and it was substantial. I wasn't the greatest author back then and my book was more like a pamphlet but the number of pages isn't what made it impactful. It wasn't an achievement because of the beautiful language or the raw emotion or the command of English throughout. No, my pamphlet, my book, my opus was necessary because it ejected me from an experiment that ran for fifty generations. (Perhaps longer, time hasn't stopped yet)

What happens when the meaty fruit of the black body is taken and harvested?

What happens when the meaty fruit of the black body is denied love?

What happens when the meaty fruit of the black body is denied pride?

What happens when the meaty fruit of the black body is denied of a history?

I remember they studied me.

I remember in second grade they wanted to measure how fast and how well I could read, my level of proficiency was recorded, and my remarkable marks were credited to cheating. My teacher placed her hand on my shoulder and told me that there was no way I could have read the passage that fast.

I remember in third grade they wanted to see how clean we were so they spanned the room checking our heads for lice and when they found none concluded that everyone who looked like me must use a special kind of shampoo. My teacher stood behind me and said it doesn't make sense that we weren't infested.

I remember learning what it means to be profiled in fifth grade. I learned that there were things that happened when no one was looking that increasingly came to resemble things that only I would do, and that only people who looked like me would do.

I remember in sixth grade I learned how institutions built for the edification of people could bind those people and bind them tighter than an enemy would. My desk was positioned strategically behind two bookshelves cattycornered away from the rear wall cutting me off from the room. My view consisted of the prison gray cinderblock wall behind me, the back of bookshelves in front of me, and the television with the blue screen displaying the time off to my side. My view changed only twice that year: once when there was a meeting with my parents and the bookshelves were miraculously removed from the corner and when I allowed to witness those planes tear down the Twin Towers.

I remember they studied me.

I remember when they told me where I came from; they only ever mentioned slave ships and plantations. I remember that none of the plantations had names unless Africans rebelled there and were defeated. I remember that none of the ships they talked about had names or captains or crews. They navigated the ghoulish oceans for months at a time floating like specters across the ocean; I speculate these ghost ships with no name and no captain may have lifted up and flown away had their bellies not been full of sweet suffering black bodies.

I remember that the Mayflower had a name and a captain and a crew and the crew had names and a home and a destination and I remember that all of that was on the test.

I remember that it began to matter where we came from and how we came to be here while our books were open but eventually we were made to turn the page and move on.

I remember they asked us to move on.

I remember that our culture was taken and sold back to us. I remember we paid with our lives and our dignity and our children and our children's children.

They stacked us on top of one another and we ate and defecated in the same space and we grew to hate. We grew to hate them and ourselves and hope because it makes disappointment worse and vision because what we imagine is impossible. They stacked us on top of one another so that we slept with the feet of our children in our mouths and then they sold our children. We grew to hate family and loss and legacy and familiarity because they make separation hurt so bad. They

Austin Vandorian Grier

stacked us on top of one another and dropped a crack bomb in the middle of their project, watching as we cycled metric tons through the tight confines of our concentration camps until we were all ghosts and the victims of ghosts.

I remember that we became accustomed to ghosts and the dead and loss and pain and sorrow and violence and depression. I remember that when we arrived we sang songs while walking on hot coals and picking white fruit in briar patches. I remember that we made new songs while walking over needles while we pushed white fruit through the veins and halls of our homes.

I remember they said that our music was the cause of troubles. Our foods were the cause of our troubles. Our clothes were the cause of our troubles. Our culture was the cause of our problem.

I remember realizing that I had not been treated. I remember the day, sitting behind those bookshelves, that I realized that all the beautiful black bodies I had ever read about or met were victims and survivors of a great and enduring mass rape.

I had seen no doctors, been administered no evaluations, attended no sessions, and received no treatment. I remember that no one spoke of the trauma.

Those beautiful black bodies were ripped from the trees they grew from in a land they thrived in, only to be crammed into the bottom of nameless ships with no captain and no crew. They lay supine in vomit and feces in the midst of the dead and those who wished they would die. If they emerged alive having not perished at the hand of starvation, or disease or violence or despair...they were met by a crowd of wolves salivating and mad. They were made to stand on pillars with no clothes, no home, no language and no hope. They were poked and prodded and harassed, dirty fingers massaged their gums and gentiles. They were sold.

I remember we were made to plough the ground and dig our own graves and then with a whip to our backs we were made to lie down on the ground we broke and civilization sprung from that beautiful black fruit. Civilization sprung from those graves but they deserved no tombstone.

Austin Vandorian Grier

I remember we survived and though we
were made to forget the names of our
country, our language, our family, the
voice of god, hope, vision, love, respect,
dignity, history and comfort…we endured.

I remember that we began to remember.
We forgot to treat our hair and hate our
skin or our circumstance. We thrust our
fists into the air and screamed that our
beautiful black fruit was power and we
believed it.

I remember they took our leaders and
replaced them with propaganda and public
school and chapters in our school books
that were ten pages long chronicling our
rape and neglecting the names of our
rapists, of their ships and captains and of
our civilizations.

I remember that we were in pain. I
remembered that we must still be in pain.
I remembered what I must have always
known.

My plight has never been my own.
My love has never been my own.
My body has never been my own.
My thoughts have never been my own.
My history has never been my own.

My image has never been my own.
My perception has never been my own.
My sorrow has never been my own.

I wrote a book when I was younger and it was substantial. It was a pivotal and groundbreaking work because it was the first time I was able to work past my trauma and take ownership of myself. I was able to own my notions and my beliefs and my convictions and I was able to narrate my own history. The years I endured of people who didn't look like me telling me who I and what I thought and what I felt was came to an abrupt end.

I allowed myself to tell my story. I allowed myself to have a history. All the ordeals I lived through were well documented, as were the ships and their captains and their crews and the places they stole me from.

I freed myself from chains that no one could see but me because our history books said they had been broken centuries ago. You can't see what you don't believe.

As soon as I was free I resolved that everything I did from then on would be a demonstration of my love and my plight as

the meaty fruit known as the black body,
recently relinquished from the lingering
grasp of the American experiment.

My intention was to exhaust all the love
and the purpose and all of the life in my
little black body.

My resolve remains the same.

The 25th Hour

I believe that there is a lifetime that exists between seconds and milliseconds and every other perceivable increment of time. It probably manifests itself as a tiny grain of forever wedged into the sensitive and eternal cogs of the everlasting.

I believe that God made the entire cosmos between heartbeats, between moments, between contractions and waves and eruptions and gasps and prayers.

I believe that when the griots whisper about the forest and the sci-fi writers type about the twilight zone that we are all talking about the same time, the same place and the same thing. The life that we live is one long extended moment that's been stretched and tied over the rim of our understanding, covering all that we know like a drum.

Therefore, we are musicians and timekeepers and lovers of rhythm and pattern and symmetry. We live in a time miniscule enough to be forgotten and just

Austin Vandorian Grier

large enough to be divided and rationed for our consumption.

Our hour was crafted and hanged on the certainty that life goes on. Our hour is small yet expansive, inconsequential yet impactful, fleeting and yet everlasting. Life is an inhale, a tick, a tock, a raindrop, a sea floor, a lightning strike and a piece of sunshine tumbling through the clouds – all frozen.

Our hour is frozen. Our hour isn't time at all because life and love and the scribbles on a page exist in a space too small for seconds, nestled just beyond our notions on the border of forever, coiled into a massless mass just bantam enough to be divided into pages.

The Shrewd, The Dragon and The Viceroy

I was born in the city; we lived on the west side – off Tuck, by the rec center. There was something very quiet about our street, but very loud. It was a protruding rock in the middle of an aggressive river, tainted but separate. I suppose I was in an ant farm. My world functioned normally enough as far as I was concerned but seemed cut off from a bigger more advanced world on the other side of the glass.

I'd sit in the backyard under our clothing line and I could see Freedom Drive on the other side of a sea of grass that mingled with my backyard before stretching out like a green landing strip towards nowhere in particular. I'd watch the cars scurry like roaches and watch the grass tickle the feet of the utility posts that straddled the field carrying miles of electric lines to the ends of the Earth. I'd stare at the highway and listen to the cars go by and if I listened long enough I didn't hear the cars at all, only my heartbeat. It was almost as if all that noise wasn't noise at all after a while, it was what quiet sounded like.

Consequently, on nights there were no sirens and I couldn't hear the traffic the silence was deafening, and I got little sleep. It wasn't until I would close my eyes, picture the highway and listen to my heartbeat that I would drift off.

Back then the highway and the Hardees sign that rose above it were the ends of the Earth and an eternity away. The view of the city beyond the highway dropped off like a cliff and I always got the feeling that there was nothing else beyond it for humans certainly God lived there. However, I could never go there, I was tethered to my house by an ethereal umbilical cord. There are, after all, forces that ground all things; for the inanimate it is gravity, for the religious it is God and for my brother and I it was our mother. My mother was our gravity. She was afraid for us and so our boundaries were definitive and precise, allowing her to see where we were at all times from our porch. Our directions were not to pass the old school two blocks to the north and not to pass Mrs. Caroline's house two houses to the south. My father, a level-headed man, seemed confident in our ability to survive outside of those boundaries and I imagine when he did become gravity it was at the beckoning of my mother. My world, for what seemed like decades, existed inside of those three blocks.

We played outside, digging in the dirt, fighting, racing in the street, playing "throw em up fuck em up" in the backyard for an eternity at a time. We were too young to place things in context and playing too hard to care and so the dirty vials by the school were anxiously collected and buried as a hidden secret treasure never to be found and the abandoned school with no children was our castle. We took no note of the chasm we were living in or the salt and pepper couple who lived on top of the hill across the street. We just barely noticed Ms. Salt running around her yard screaming for help or Mr. Pepper dragging her back inside. I recall the years before I went to grade school very vividly with the bigness of the world leaving quite an impression on me. I remember when it first occurred to me that there were cities outside of my city and streets beyond my street. The streets that had been paved beyond my mother's gravity seemed dark and ominous. I was tempted to go there but too afraid to go without my brother, whose preoccupation with racing and football seemed of cure him of curiosity. I was smaller than him, round and asthmatic, possessing no athletic prowess, and lacking the luxury of being distracted. I focused daily on what could be out there. Oftentimes, I thought about it so hard and long that I'd fall asleep right where I was, overwhelmed, only to be awakened abruptly with reports that my father said to come home.

When my father called I ran home. He wasn't a large man, compared to other men that I'd seen but being my dad made him bigger. There was a thick air of responsibility that surrounded him, a responsibility I couldn't understand but one that I could feel. The feeling that I got when he came home was a testament to his size. When his car pulled into the driveway my brother and I would race to hide as if there was an intruder about to break in and after my father had crossed the threshold and we were sure that our mother had given no reports that would require a whipping we'd run out to greet him. On days my mother gave an unfavorable report we couldn't stay hidden long enough. The worst part of the punishments that followed a bad report had little to do with the physical pain, and more to do with the betrayal. Most children forget they were punished after a few hours, content and emerging from under the pillows they had buried themselves under but I never forgot. I could never fathom the audacity that it'd take to be my friend (back then being friendly meant we were friends) and then spank me. My love never wavered but I struggled with how that love was supposed to be displayed. I remember looking at my father's hand and having mixed feelings of fear and adoration.

There wasn't anything bigger than my father's hands and I wanted to be just like him. I would stare at my hands for hours as if to will them into growing, when that inevitably failed, I settled for examining his. When we sat on the couch, to watch football or play horsey, his hand often covered my entire torso. I'd marvel at how long his fingers were, how big his palms were, how much stronger he was than I. I wanted to be close to him when I thought about his hands and for him to be happy with me. I wasn't sure how but I knew he protected me and I'm not sure what was haunting me but I felt safer with him. His energy, that very specific air about him, didn't go unnoticed by everyone else. The skeletons that sat on porches watching while we played in the street, rarely speaking, came to life when he came outside. They called out to him, flailing their arms. I suppose they wanted his attention just like I wanted it; the kind of attention I craved when he put my brother and I down for naps while football was on. They called out to him and he would wave his huge hand and they would seem satisfied retreating back into their petrified state, perhaps feeling safer now that he had acknowledged them. I knew that feeling well. I knew that if my father could see me, or if I could see him, that I was safe and so whenever I felt uneasy I'd go and sneak a peek at him. When I had confirmed that he was still there, watching television or sleeping or cooking…I would return to what I was doing before safe and reassured.

When my father wasn't there to protect me there was my brother. My brother is two years my senior and was my social guardian. He was a hall pass of sorts, my permission to play in the game or to be invited into a friend's house. He was fast, so he was popular and he wouldn't leave me and they wanted him, so naturally they accepted me. His presence validated mine and that made me feel welcomed.

The neighborhood kids looked at him like the skeletons looked at my father. My brother and my father share that quality, they carry with them an air that saturates the room…though neither of them is large in stature you'd follow them before they would follow you. I was no different, I would follow my brother to the ends of the Earth had he ever suggested it but he didn't because he was busy racing. I'm certain he never noticed but I took great pride in trying my hardest to beat him home for dinner and losing by large margins.

We were children and our social hierarchy reflected our lack of insight, experience and resources. For dirty little hood kids there weren't have's and have not's because we all had very little. There were no tax brackets, no examination of socioeconomic conditions or adjusted incomes. The only thing that mattered was if you could fight and run. Early on I could do neither and I relied heavily on my brother to make up for where I lacked. I graciously allowed him to fight my fights and shamelessly sauntered into the winner's circle with him after he had won a race. As we grew older his ability and willingness to compensate for my flat-footed performance began to dissipate and that welcoming feeling that I had come to rely on disappeared. My parents were preoccupied with the twins they had just brought home not too long ago. I felt alone, but not the type of alone that haunts people and chips away at them but a tailored loneliness as if I were created to be this way. My brother was off racing or tackling, my father was at work and my mother was inside with the twins, left to my own vices I'd sit in the driveway and stare at the huge tree in the front yard thinking to myself "we are just alike."

I was a happy child, easily pleased. Even back then I don't think I spent a lot of time dealing with reality, instead I was immersed in dark, imaginary figments that comforted me like being buried in a mother's chest during hugs, hugs that generally followed me falling and injuring myself. The things I imagined were very real to me. Everyday my hands seemed bigger after having stared at them. I truly believed that believing made it so. I thought that underlining sentences in a book was equivalent to writing and so I had authored many books by the time I actually learned how to read. My impulses were also very real; they seemed not to be impulses at all but mandates.

One day while walking down the hall in my house it occurred to me that I had never seen a wall as big and white and pure and inviting as this one. My moment of clarity was rattling and exciting almost as if I had discovered this wall hidden behind the wall we all knew. I stared at the wall salivating, I wanted to draw on it, to paint on it, to cover ever inch with color but I was afraid. I decided that it was a bad idea to draw on the wall and retired to my room to author more books but the wall continued to call me like the Sirens. I don't remember grabbing the lipstick from its resting place on my mother's dresser, I only remember standing in front of the wall with it in my hand and a voice in my ear. The same voice that called me - urged me, gushing about how beautiful our painting could be. I couldn't muster up the courage to draw and so instead I paced making sure there was no sign of my parents and when I saw no one around to stop me I could no longer resist. I fixated on the wall and began, feverishly; I began to etch a red dragon with bold lines I tattooed my home. I imagined that I wasn't holding lipstick at all but a flame and I branded my dragon into the wall as fast as I could. The fear that I had when I was pacing had been swallowed by a voice urging me to let this dragon loose in the hallway. I was just finishing my masterpiece when my father rounded the corner. The voice I had heard, raspy and seductive, completely disappeared and the feverish passion I felt only moments before melted and they were replaced by cold, damp helplessness. I was overrun with fear and a deep sorrow, fear that my punishment would come swiftly but last forever and deep sadness that my father wouldn't believe or understand that it wasn't me who drew that picture. Hell, drawing the picture wasn't even my idea. When I finally found words all I could muster was "taa daa" hoping he might be pleased. I cried, "It wasn't me" when I got my whipping and my fears were confirmed, my father seemed only to get angrier. When it was over and I was made to slay my dragon with soap and water there was no voice cheering me on, and no fire in my stomach compelling me to keep going, only silence.

Afterwards, I melted into my pillows and my writhing turned the little space I occupied under the cover into a steamy, electrified lagoon. I was hurt and confused and remorseful and bitter and rubbing the welts on my thighs though it caused pain. I'm sure I cried only a few moments before the fatigue of being hyper-emotional caught up with me and lulled me to sleep.

I don't remember feeling any pain before I birthed that dragon, though I'm sure I felt pain before my epiphany I was not aware that it was something that could be identified and separated from all the things that are, that exist. My consciousness was panoramic; a large picture of everything, where nothing was more itself than it was anything else. Much like memories, things that stood alone seemed to bleed into one another and it was hard to tell one thing from the other. When I sat under that big tree in our front yard if I held my little hand up long enough my pudgy fingers stopped being fingers altogether and became branches instead.

For a long time everything was the same, the extreme safety that I felt in the presence of my brother was synonymous with the comfort I got from hearing sirens and traffic at bedtime. The gravity of my mother's authority was no different than the highway off in the distance that landlocked us. However, pain changed all that...it fragmented my ideas and splintered my notions and feelings and I was torn. I realized almost all at once that my mother could protect me from what was beyond the school but was nowhere to be found when my father disciplined me. My brother's social superiority was infantile in our house and no matter how much I needed him in the house he was only capable of protecting me outside. My father's hands were huge and magical when we were playing but they were inescapable and frightening when I was in trouble. I imagine that when Prometheus came down that mountain to enlighten the people that he brought them pain to cook their raw meat with. My ability to discern burgeoned in response to the sting of punishment and misfortune. I saw the friend I had in my father evaporated when he saw my dragon on the wall; the stark difference in his posture and tone was something that needed remembering. If I ever forgot what it felt like to be standing in that hall all alone with nothing but a tube of lipstick and an imaginary dragon to protect me I may be doomed to live cyclically birthing and slaying dragons and subsequently crying myself to sleep in the bed I made.

That voice and the dragon it birthed
earned me the first scar I can identify.
Pain is sobering. The burning you feel
when remorseful, the sting when cornered,
the stabbing when betrayed all separate
what we believe from what actually exists.
The images I had projected on the green
screen of reality caught fire and fell into a
heap of ash and from that ash crawled the
phoenix of experience, wobbling and
unsure of itself. Pain saved my life. The
scar on my consciousness rested like
bifocals magnifying what had been
invisible to me. The Earth became
fragmented, splintered, fractured,
shattered and things were more as they
were and less how I imagined them.
Those free of these kinds of scars, though
content, are doomed to mistake a lack of
sadness for an abundance of joy.

Life and all that it has to teach us rolls out
green and flat and we run across it, that's
our experience. We crawl and stumble and
eventually run, and all that time we have
the good fortune of learning. I suppose we
learn greater lessons from thorns than
roses. We will eventually chase butterflies
through that field amazed at how the sun
seems to set its wings on fire and that

butterfly is the same as happiness and
security and love.

Having lived a life absent of thorns and
dragons we may believe that what we see
is all there is to see and how we see may
be the only form of sight. Our vision may
be impaired and our discernment
diminished. God bless us if our Truman
Burbank bubbles have protected us from
knowing better; bless us if we are destined
to chase butterflies over this flat green
mistaking the Viceroy for the Monarch for
we have yet to feel pain and thus cannot
avoid it. Amen.

Knowing

it's hard to rest when you know things,
spiraling things that coil and hang from the
rafters drooping just low enough to tease
the tip of my consciousness only to slither
back and I feel what I can't see and see
what I cannot make out and think what I
can't even whisper but I know, I know
things…wet things that coat it all in a thin
layer of things to come

a slimy chromatic film

and

I know enough to know that I don't know
much, just enough to know that I don't
know enough and it keeps me up and
when I sleep I dream of wanting to wake
but never waking up.

Austin Vandorian Grier

Rods

we creep, sometimes slowly and often
quickly and feverishly out of the darkness
on our bellies hungry and wanting and
needing to be seen and acknowledged
and having our names known and the
shadowy anonymity that we escaped from
is hell compared to the sun on our skin

there's the radiant energy that warms our
faces when our faces are known in places
and we bask in it and thrive and bloom and
glow and while we dance we neglect to
look around and soon we are surrounded
by people we do not know, people who
cannot see our glow and we are back in
hell

and we creep once more

and they acknowledge that we were once
illuminated and they ask if we can bring
back the light and we realize we have not
changed or dimmed and they have
adjusted and we are no longer so bright

Cones

I suppose the issue is the few things in this world that are certain all suppositions at best...what we believe to be can never be any degree less than what is because we are what we think and we can't be less than what is because then nothing is real...or maybe we are not real and nothing can done and nothing can be gained or attained or lost and we are lost and wandering and we cannot see and it's all the same...I hope, in strength or conviction, that supposing rivals knowing because knowing seems absolute and none of us fleshy things are really ever sure about anything but maybe if we pray there may come a day when we'll see shades and we'll know truth and we'll know, opposed to supposing, that what may be more important than a color is it's hue.

Austin Vandorian Grier

The Death Of The HBCU

How do you introduce the elephant in the room?

You call it by its name.

Death. Demise. Decline. Disease.
Dissolve. Atrophy. Degenerate.

Black colleges and universities are second only to the black church as vehicles for the advancement of people of color. They rose from blood stained dirt as monuments to our potential and opened their doors to us when all other doors were sealed. They afforded us the opportunity to learn about where we came from and about where we were going. They made us heroes, nurturing and producing our greatest practitioners who came to aid of a nation that hated them and a people who depended on them. We rallied behind our heroes. We rallied behind the cause. We rallied around our rights (or a lack thereof). We did not rally behind our institutions. We fed legends to our children about the campus. We fed them legends about what we did and how it changed the world. We fed them legends about the movement and how we came to be here. We forgot to feed them purpose. Why are we here? What are we supposed to do now that we can eat where we want and vote? Who are we supposed to do it for? How are our people and our institutions affected when we do not do our part? We forgot to task them. We forgot to tell them that after you build it you have to maintain it. Our conversations went from going off to school so you could come back to your community as an asset and help it flourish –to- going off to school because that's what you do after high school. We went from chasing decent paying jobs so that we could pump money and resources back into our communities and our monuments –to- chasing jobs as a means to move far away and pay back loans. We failed to acknowledge that even the best systems couldn't put out if nothing was put in. We carried on this this way for decades, sending our children off to school so they can get jobs and recalling our fondest college memories while forgetting to give back as alumni. We traveled back for our homecomings but failed to come home otherwise. We believed that as long as students enrolled in our schools they would continue to thrive.

Then one day we look up and to our surprise we're all in the same room and it's crowed and it's hot and it's uncomfortable. There's an elephant in the corner, a disgustingly immense protruding monolith of pungent flesh and it just so happens to be taking up all the space. However, none of us can see it and if we can see it we pretend that we can't or we acknowledge that's its there but feel powerless to remove it. We're all standing inside the walls of our beloved institutions, poised either to reinforce its walls or to allow it collapse on top of us. The stories that we told about the glory days fail to mask the smell of decay and soon we are all thinking the same thing. There's an elephant in the room. How do we introduce it? How do we address it? How do we shed light?

We call it by its name.

Its name is a lack of scholarship dollars due to lack in alumni giving.

Its name is majors that do not prepare students for entry-level jobs in their field.

Its name is decreases in retention due to a lack of student preparedness and motivation.

Its name is highly qualified students and student athletes attending predominantly white institutions at an alarming rate.

Its name is stricter qualification for parent plus loans.

Its name is the exponential growth of college costs in response to the introduction of the Pell Grant and then the subsequent cuts in Pell Grant dollars.

Its name is the miniscule social footprints our institutions make.

Its name is a focus on institution size opposed to the quality of the product.

Its name is a failure to acknowledge and adapt to changes in the labor market and financial climate we live in.

Its name is a failure on the part of our people to rally around the education of our children starting at birth.

Its name is a preoccupation with our personal ambitions opposed to aspiring to serve and build our communities.

Its name is a culture that creates a correlation between leaving and never coming back with success.

Its name is college students with elementary goals.

And then someone raises their voice and asks, "What do we do about it? We can't possibly support our institution or pull our resources before tackling the issue that has us pinned down." They say, "we always talk about what's wrong but we need action, we need to do something because sitting around discussing our problems isn't going to help."

And here I submit my response. I don't have a comprehensive solution to our elephant but I have a starting place. We have to start with an admission.

I am sick.
I do not feel well.
I am sick.
Something is not right.

Things are not working as well as they used to.
At one point I could and now I find that I cannot.
I am sick.

The time has come for us to become the practitioners that our heroes once were. We now have the responsibility of doctoring our institutions and moving them away from extinction and towards maximizing their potential. We (black people) have a habit of acting like everything is ok when its not and behaving as if admitting *things aren't going as well as they could be* is also an admission of defeat.

We have to start by saying that our institutions are not what they once were. Their reach is greater than ever and yet we touch less people. Our systems, curriculums and practices are more sophisticated and yet we are less prepared. We have substantially grown our number of graduates but there hasn't been a substantial increase in alumni giving.

Austin Vandorian Grier

As soon as we can admit that there is an issue as a people we are a third of the way there.

The second stage of treatment is to find out what is wrong (usually by examining symptoms). After we acknowledge that something isn't right we can now have dialogue about what is wrong specifically. Because we're practitioners we often look to symptoms to point us to the problem. However, I believe that a large part of our current predicament is our fixation on this stage of treatment (problem solving). I believe that our sicknesses persist as a testimony, not of the tenacity and stamina of our illness, but of our preoccupation with symptoms. We are results driven and also products of the microwave generation. That combination of phenomena creates a problem solver who will focus on the quick fix, the problem solver who waters down dismal retention figures by increasing admissions to the institution. That type of approach doesn't address why retention was low in the first place and later that problem resurfaces in the midst of a larger student population and a third of a class not returning to school (based on a true story).

We must look at symptoms as a means to understand the issue but resist the temptation to treat symptoms alone. When retention rates are low we don't just want to tinker with numbers, we want to know why. When our students aren't getting hired we don't just have bigger career fairs, we need to find out why they aren't being hired. When our students aren't giving back we don't need to increase the number of cold calls made asking for donations, we need to find out why they aren't giving back. Treat the symptoms but don't forget the illness.

The third stage of treatment involves treatment and prognosis, what are we going to do now and what should we do in the future (as it pertains to our illness). I've categorized my solutions into two categories: synergy and community. The world we live in now requires that we move with a combined strength that is cutting edge. Those themes will be reoccurring because almost every problem I can identify could be alleviated with our combined strength or by updating our current practices to more productive models. The two approaches can almost be used interchangeably but they differ where synergy focuses on know-how and

community focuses on how we allocate
and utilize our human resources.

Synergy

It's rarely about what you do and more
about how you do it. If you're a runner in a
race and you want to win you have to
acknowledge that it isn't just about
running, it's about running fast and if you
can help it it's about running the fastest.
Our approach to a lot of our goals, such as
career preparation and retention, focus on
doing the right things but not necessarily
doing the right things well. The difference
between the two is the difference between
running and running fast. Our students
can't just be afforded the opportunity to
learn about their field (running), they have
to be taught specific skills and industry
practices (running fast). Imagine the
employment rate of a business department
that doesn't graduate business majors but
financial/business analyst or a political
science department that didn't just
graduate political science majors but
functioning paralegals. These aren't quick
fixes, they would take time but general
knowledge is good for the soul but not the

job market. That's a trend our institutions have to adapt to.

Our majors also have to incorporate an interdisciplinary approach. I graduated with a degree in political science and I was only required to take one professional level finance/business course. If I relied solely on my degree I'd be unable to contribute to discourse about campaign contributions, the effects of financial trends on policy, the effect of policy on the financial climate and finances as an element of our governments foreign and domestic interests. What's problematic is that those talking points are what I'd need to even be considered for an entry-level political analyst position. We have to encourage students and faculty to blend their interest and expertise to produce a new cutting edge student and a more valuable and multifaceted faculty member.

Our employed graduates are also our best source of information pertaining to being a young professional. We often contract speakers and presenters that our students do not know and do not connect with when we have alumni who are just as qualified to share. Currently student organizations hold and facilitate seminars about how to be successful professionals (having never been successful professionals) while successful professional alumni could be called on to do the job. Our alumni have to be tapped into for more than money. Their expertise is the cutting edge that a lot of our students need, especially in regard to industry specific knowledge.

Synergy is making sure that we use information itself and the sources of information at our disposal in the most efficient manner possible to maximize our potential and move from producing competitors who can just run to producing competitors who can run fast.

Community

It takes a village. Our schools are our children. Our students are our children. Our legacies are our children. It will take all of us to take care of what is ours, to raise and nurture our children. We have not (for a long time now) effectively used our community. We have produced teachers and doctors and athletes, parents, DJ's, production managers, photographers, graphic designers, police officers, lawyers, judges, business analyst, computer technicians, programmers and nurses and at most have asked them for money. We have to create a culture where showing your face is worth more than your money. The opportunities for tutoring, mentorship, internships, employment and vast increases in school spirit is unlimited if we begin to look at one another as assets opposed to treating money as the only meaningful contribution that one can make.

Though I believe there is more than one type of meaningful contribution there's no dodging the fact that money makes the world spin. Imagine if every living alumnus of our institutions gave $5 a year, would the condition of our schools be better? Imagine institutions that didn't rely so heavily on government funding and thus didn't have to cut quality programs every time the economy or a politician took a nosedive (times when quality programs are most needed). We also can't overlook the need for transparency since that's a major issue when it comes to donations and rightfully so. If I give my hard-earned money I want to know where it goes. There would have to be a way that people can track their dollars and see how they're working. The whole concept of asking one who passed through the halls of our schools to give a little back to help the next person and taking the time to tell them specifically how their dollar helped is the root of any successful fundraising campaign and it is also a great stimulus to notions such as community and social responsibility.

Another portion of community has to do with the members of our community who do not go to our schools. Imagine if your favorite basketball or football player had attended your school and affected your schools athletic program? Imagine if our brightest came to our schools and raised the epistemic standard? The obvious argument is that these students want to go to the most reputable schools and while that's understandable it seems a little more substantial to help a school become reputable than to attend one just because its already seen that way. Our sense of community has to include what we do on behalf of our community. Imagine if all black players went to black colleges and universities, what would their revenues look like? In turn, what would their facilities look like? Their school spirit? Their student body? Their faculty? The change has to start somewhere. We have to make it a point to teach that responsibility to our young stars, fame and money will come if you're great but should you have to forgo your institutions to succeed?

Our leadership should also be based in the community. I envision alumni boards that exist in equity to the Board of Trustees at our institutions, which would consist of members who are chosen by the student body forcing leadership to interact with the student. I realize the alumni associations exist but I am weary of them because I feel they often act in the best interest of the alumni and not the best interest of the institution. I would not want decisions made for our institutions by people who cannot be held accountable by the students.

The last portion of community is perhaps the most pivotal. We have to be able to criticize one another. We often talk about unity and working together and moving forward collectively, rhetoric designed to encourage us to work together. The part of unity that we never mention is uniformity. The world we live in is increasingly diverse, everything varies...where we come from, what/how we think, how we view ourselves, how we view others, what we identify as our goals etc. The days when we were all united under one banner pushing toward a common goal are long gone. This is not a popular topic in our hyper-individualistic society. No one wants to be anything like the next person; everyone wants to exert themselves as a unique body (which is honorable). However, every successful movement in the history of movements was homogeneous (in regard to core ideology not necessarily methodology). We can't move forward as a generation when the individuals who make up our generation are preoccupied with their personal struggles. That's not to say that we shouldn't take care of home first but we can't fight so hard for ourselves that we forget the community we live in. The rift between self-actualization and the realization of our collective goals is the source of most of the criticisms that we've either furnished or endured.

When my dad used to lecture me about sagging my pants I imagine it was less about wanting to stifle my self-expression and more about our collective prosperity. Perhaps his disdain was rooted in our collective goal to keep our young men from being victims of the prison industrial complex. Perhaps his disdain was rooted in the fact that the world perceived my harmless sagging as an indication that I was already a victim of our penal system or that soon I would be. Perhaps his disdain was rooted in the fear that I may adopt societies view of me (a common occurrence among black men) and that I may willingly and happily throw me life away through drugs or violence. I pushed back because I thought that he was being hateful but in retrospect he was attempting to push me back under the banner. He was attempting to push me back under a banner we could all walk under and fight for. My personal expression not only ostracized me but it also made a danger to the movement started to advance me. I could (my expression) be used as evidence that our movement is meaningless. This has been done countless times over throughout our history…the slaves who told when others ran, the protesters that used violence during non-violent demonstrations, the men who used their guns on their people instead of the police we stockpiled the weapons for.

We have to be able to push one another back under the banner. The problem is that in this modern society everything is ok, everything goes and everything is acceptable. Not only is it ok, its taboo to be critical of others (apparently because we all have flaws). Apparently, if I've ever made a mistake I'm in no position to share my thoughts or to disagree with the actions of my peers. I haven't been bombarded into insensitivity or obliviousness by popular culture, nor have I been lulled by the temptation to limit all criticism to hate and intolerance. When the sharing of opinions is an infringement on rights we are doomed. We have to be able to be corrected. Everything can be done in love, bring criticism back. Bring being critical back. Bring back discernment. Being judgmental is the mark of an intelligent person not a villain. What we should be working to eliminate is condemnation. We are a community and in the event you represent us and what you're doing isn't in OUR best interest you will hear about it. That's a promise and that's how it should be (that goes for perpetrators and naysayers).

Our problems are rooted in the fragmentation of our resources, specifically our alumni and their expertise. We won't be able to move forward without pulling together and clearly defining the issues and their solutions. In the event that we decide not to acknowledge where we are and what we should be doing our institutions will close and all we will have left is the stories we've told.

Treat the illness; do not become preoccupied with symptoms.

Call the illness by its name.
Make sure that solutions are specific, measurable, achievable, relevant and time-bound (SMART)

From a real place,

AV

Austin Vandorian Grier

Death

there were things we could not account for

like

why a punctured vessel swells like the tide
in the dead of night crawling up the coast
towards the moon

and

the waves of breath pause...no longer
pulled by the moonlight that once brought
us to life beginning at dusk

and

what was warm is now cold and what was
cold is now warm and burning and broken
and hurting

and

the pain shoots like stars through the part
of us that wishes with every grain of salt in
the sea that the ocean wasn't standing still

Regret

there is a specific note that rings out, a metallic echoing, reverberating during libation when I pour recollections from my wide mouth mason jar...they fall like rain from the sky of places I had dared to go, drumming, into an empty basin of places I wish I had gone and the sound bubbles up into a feverish steam that thickens the air and pressures the walls to perspire...the sweat beads and begins to run converging into veins that run sour like estuaries into a sea of quicksand that churns at my calves and when I try to run my feet crush my shame and force from it what will soon be the wine of my remorse and when I find there is no escape I settle for a drink, lowering my mason jar to sample the fermented pain and I sip it deeply and pour out the rest in memory of what I cannot forget only to be greeted by that specific note.

Austin Vandorian Grier

Perch

I was a flower once, retreated so far into
myself that my blooms were roots and
what would have been my roots prior to
my world turning over were gentle perches
for the crows and I'd shiver and glow and
grow when the moonlight of the unrequited
streaked and slithered its way through the
darkness and cold, then it would force the
dirt to ebb and flow like a moody ocean
making way for my mushroom

From Whence Cometh My Yoke

It goes a long way back, some twenty years. All my life I had been looking for something, and everywhere I turned someone tried to tell me what it was. I accepted their answers too, though they were often in contradiction and even self-contradictory. I was naive. I was looking for God and asking everyone except God questions, which God, and only God, could answer. It took me a long time and much painful boomeranging of my expectations to achieve a realization everyone else appears to have been born with: That I am nobody until my maker can see me. But first I had to discover that I was an invisible man!

~ ~ ~

The cloaked man walked with a distinct urgency, the kind of quickened pace that you recognize from across the square and yet he was a stranger to me. His back was to me and he seemed to be gaining ground faster than ground could appear in front of him. He could have been floating if man were capable of such a thing but he left no footprints and his footfalls made no noise and his cloak did not sway in the wind as he pressed forward toward the mountain. I clamored behind him. I ran with all my strength panicking at the thought of letting him out of my sight, not knowing why I needed to keep up with him. I ran and clawed as the ground stretched in front of me tripling the gap between us and pushing the man to the bottom of the mountain, he began to scale it. I was yelling but there was no sound and crying but there were no tears and I was running but gaining no ground and the man was climbing. I looked on helplessly as my anxiety climbed in step with the stranger. He seemed to know where to step and the mountain seemed to offer him limb after to limb like an eager lover and he climbed higher still. When he reached the top he slipped over the lip of the monolith out of sight. I let out a howl of despair against my will, as I always did, just as lightening struck the peak. At that moment a wave of lava surged over the peak spilling into the valley where I stood and it ran down the mountainous alter like sacrificial blood. I turned to run but my feet were beneath the surface and I stood helplessly as the lava galloped toward me burning the ground and melting all the rocks. When the time came for me to face the flaming sea it stopped an arms-length in front of me and erected itself, a large smoldering wall. I saw my reflection in the wall and when I reached out to myself for help I was burned alive as I watched.

I awoke in frenzy. My arms were flailing and I rolled out of bed screaming and writhing in pain, everything was hot and I was on fire. My mother dashed through the partition separating my quarters from the rest of the cabin. She put both of her hands on my face, the tips of her middle fingers pressed into my temple, and hissed my name. I was immediately extinguished as I came to myself and I collapsed damp and emancipated on her bosom sweating and fatigued from my night terror.

That same dream had crept into my sleep since I was a child. In my primary years I was thought to be sickly and weak. My eyes were a rare black and my sockets were sunk deep into my skull. The mages believed that I would die young at the hand of disease or a mountain cat that may run away with my frail frame. Consequently, I was not schooled with the other children nor was I allowed much interaction with them. I spent all of my time at home with my mother and my tutor. He was an outcast from some land far away who prided himself on knowing a bit about everything. He lived with us and taught me in exchange for shelter. I learned from him what all of the children learned about, how we came to be here in this appointed place and what we were appointed to do and the manner in which we were instructed to do it. My tutor mused daily about what great fortune it is to have been born in a place where every man could be a God through the work of his back and the sweat of his brow. I was always troubled by the thought that we were anything like the Gods I had heard of in the rumors that slithered around the village; I was always especially disturbed when considering the notion that we could be Gods while simultaneously acknowledging the reality of my sickly build. On the rare occasion that I unwittingly allowed my skepticism to show on my face he would go into a dramatic rendition of our narrative.

There was once a father with two sons. The younger son, unlike his brother, was energetic and haughty and a lover of adventure. One day he asked his father for his part of the estate. His father divided his property and gifted his son with his proper portion. The son then went off to another country where he found a valley that he liked and he settled there. His living was wild and excessive and he rolled around in his money and women from the sun's rise to the sun's set. Almost all at once his money was gone and the son was left hungry and penniless. The son fearing for his life and dying from hunger hired himself out to a local dignitary as a servant. As a reward for his hard work he was allowed to sleep with the cattle and eat from the troughs with the pigs. Now everyday instead of rolling around in women he rolled around in mud and the dirt hid his tears.

One day while the son slept on a bale of hay God came to him in a dream and he stood before him with a flaming blade. God spoke to him and his words cracked the ground. The son trembled and screamed and tried to run but all around him the Earth had fallen away. God spoke to him saying "Why do you run from the one who came to free you?" The son asked God "Am I not free?" and God answered, "You believe that you are here because you choose to be but you are foolish and proud." God stretched out the sword and cut the pride from the son's body and then reattached the son to himself. When the son woke up he thought to himself, "How many of my father's hired servants have food to spare, and here I am starving to death! I will set out and go back to my father and say to him: Father, I have sinned against heaven and against you. I am no longer worthy to be called your son; make me like one of your hired servants." The son set off toward home and he came to a great mountain. As a he began to climb the mountain one of the servants from the dignitary's house called to him saying, "Where will you go with no money and no name?" To this the son replied, "Go and tell everyone who will listen that if only man will shed his pride and climb his mountain he will again be one with God" and then he turned and climbed his mountain.

The story goes that after reaching the top of his mountain that son saw his father far off and he ran down to him and was elevated. The servant from the dignitary's house ran back to village and told everyone of the man with no money and no name who had shed his pride and climbed his mountain. He told everyone who would listen that if you reached the top you would be reunited with your father and elevated. The story spread through the village like a fever and all of the servants who rolled around in the mud huddled together laughing and dreaming of becoming God. The following day they stampeded toward the mountain and a sea of dignitaries and their hired mercenaries greeted them when they arrived. There was a public decree that no man shall scale this mountain as long as man walked the earth and fowl filled the sky.

At the end of the story my tutor would always check my face for any signs that I may have believed him and like always I was unconvinced. He would then remind me that to this day we were forbidden to climb Mount Apotheosis and that any attempt would be rewarded with crucifixion in the middle of our village, Superbian Valley.

My mother was always quick to wake me when I had my nightmares lest anyone overhear me and she made me swear not to ever tell anyone for fear that my visions might be interpreted as treason. I would never admit it to her but I thought about the top of that mountain all day and all night. It consumed all of my thoughts; I was drawn to it, pulled by it, controlled by it. When I ate I sat by the window so I could see it and when I was made to go into the village I took whichever route allowed me to get closest to it. My limbs would reach for it without my permission and my heart would quicken at the thought of it.

One night after my mother jerked me from another one of my nightmares I sat awake on my bed next to the window. The moonlight glared through my window and lit the throughway outside like it was daytime. I was staring absently at the shadow of the mountain when I saw a man walking briskly toward it. The cloaked man walked with a distinct urgency, the kind of quickened pace that you recognize from across the square or a dream and yet he was a stranger to me. His back was to me and he seemed to be gaining ground faster than ground could appear in front of him. He could have been floating if man were capable of such a thing but he left no footprints and his footfalls made no noise and his cloak did not sway in the wind as he pressed forward toward the mountain. I slipped through my window and clamored behind him. I ran with all my strength panicking at the thought of letting him out of my sight, knowing that I would never see him again if I let him out of my sight. I sprinted but his pace seemed to triple the distance between us. By the time I reached the base of the mountain the cloaked man had already climbed far ahead of me and he dipped in and out of sight on the ledges. I looked around and the centuries that would normally be keeping guard were nowhere to be found. With no one to stop me I began to climb. I climbed and time slipped away from me until I could no longer tell how long it had been but my arms and legs did not tire. By the time I reached the top it was almost dawn. I lifted myself over the lip of the mountain and I expected to see the cloaked man but I found only a clearing with a modest shrub in the middle. I walked toward it and when I stepped off the grass onto the bare ground that circled the shrub like a rash the shrug came alive and engulfed itself in blue flames. I turned to run but my feet were beneath the ground and I was trapped and then the bush spoke to me.

This is hallowed ground remove your sandals.

Austin Vandorian Grier

I looked down and I could see my feet again and so trembling I removed my sandals. I turned back to the flame and asked, "Who are you?"

I saw the beginning of time as I have seen you; I am the eternal.

Where did the cloaked man go?

There was no man; you have only seen yourself seek your source.

The man I saw wasn't real?

Before now you have lived outside the will of your creator and your spirit and body have suffered much because of it. My children have cut themselves off from me and as a result their bodies become weak and their spirits are tormented. They become filled with pride and greed and they bow their heads in front of gilded calves. You saw a soul that has grown too weary to be without its source any longer.

Are you the source?

I saw the beginning of time as I have seen you; I am the eternal.

Are you going to make me a God?

You have come seeking a reward where there is only work.

What work is there for a sickly boy like me?

You have not lived within my sight and so you have known only darkness. You have known only lands where suffering is in the valley and reward is in the mountaintop. You have known only that men with armies rule and those without the heart or might to fight bow in defeat. You have not known that you were made. You have not known humility, nor do you know me. Today I see you for the first time. Today you are not are not invisible and so there is work for you to do. You will go and pull my children into my sight. Today they toil but they do not know me so they toil in vain. Today they seek this mountaintop because they do not know that there is only pain here. There is no reward here. The reward is at the base of this mountain. What you will receive here is heavier than anything you could have picked up in ignorance. Today I see you and so you live in the light and you know that the burden is at the top of the mountain and by the sweat of your brow you will earn your reward in the valley you came from. You will be persecuted but you will never be invisible again. Go.

And what am I to tell them?

I will give you words and you will have your reward.

From On The Mountain 1

The word as it has been given to me from where I received it.

~~~

The Good Steward

1 Is there a good shepherd who hides from his flock? 2 How can the shepherd continue to be a shepherd without his sheep and his staff and his route and his destination and his problems? Is his virtue not in being a shepherd? 3 His trials are a colorful cloak woven with him in mind and tailored to his build. 4 His build suits him and his trials are forged and fitted like the horseshoe on a mare.

5 Therefore, I submit to you do not run from responsibility. Your creator has carved you from the mud and given you dominion over your space and your circumstance and your mind and your person. 6 You have done well when you have served as a diligent steward of what has been afforded to you. And so you were created with your responsibility in mind and your

talents gifted to you in proportion to what has been asked of you.

[7] You have been seeded with curiosity and skepticism and doubt so that you might seek his face and your purpose. [8] Seeded so that you will come to lean on the fruits of your labor and the faith you have employed. [9] Go and seek out opportunity and responsibility and multiply your talents. Increase your burden so that you may also increase your blessing.

[10] You are the sweet black fruit of your maker and your trials are the winepress. [11] The potency of the wine will mirror the fruit and the volume of the wine will reflect the weight and persistence of the press. [12] After a good life there shall be no wine left to be collected and there will be libations. [13] You will be gifted in accordance to your trials so toil endlessly for good but do not hope for more, instead look to the mountain for greater.

Jonah's Fish

they scorch the earth looking for a foxhole
to disappear into when they are sought
after, hunted by one thing

or another

man can't run from what he's made of you
know – ashes to ashes and all

but

man wouldn't be man if he didn't try to
duck under providence and dash past
authority only to find himself under a
restless stone on the omnipotent's stoop

Austin Vandorian Grier

For Which There Is No Cure

Previously printed in Free Samples by Jonathan Jackson

It's a hazy morning as I merge onto the expressway…the clouds hang low (*they don't care for Mondays either*) and having failed to work up the motivation to get out of bed they roll around and mute all colors leaving the highway gray and hushed. The traffic, though sparse, creeps along like metal slugs on concrete branches and the white lines on the street seems to bend under their weight. I'm in no hurry to get to work but I speed anyway, cutting fine lines as I pass, I scalpel through the thoroughfare cutting the time of my commute. Every morning I practice this frenzied, self-induced hypnosis where every car I pass is a swoop on a pendulum that brings with it the thick fog of habit and familiarity. By the time I've passed my sixth car I'm no longer driving, I'm in the passenger seat watching myself dodge and weave and it rarely occurs to me after this point in my commute that there is a world outside of my car that operates differently than I do. The rest of the world surely feels as I do and thinks as I do and exists as I do, surely they rush to places they don't want to go and believe that better is always best and surely they hate Mondays. I presume it was impulse that caused me to reach out and switch on the radio that morning. I'm not particularly sure whether I was commissioned by God or compelled by synapses or if they are one and the same (*I believe that's being hotly debated*) but either way I was led and as the speakers came to life so did my consciousness.

A stoic voice crept out of the speakers and coated the air in the car. His resolve was calm and dark but compassionate and enduring. I learned as I listened that there was a deadly breakout of Ebola in West Africa (*as if there is a such thing as a mild breakout of such a disease*) and that hundreds were suffering. The disease, which causes fever, vomiting, diarrhea and severe internal hemorrhaging, was first found in the 1970's in what was then Zaire and is now the Democratic Republic of Congo. The outbreak stretches over three countries in Africa: Guinea, Sierra Leone and Liberia (*a distance equivalent to a commute from Baltimore to Boston*) and has infected a total of 888 people and killed 539 since the beginning of the scourge in February. Making matters worse in the region is what I would come to understand a lethal duality, two-pronged pitchfork comprised of mature infrastructure in West Africa and well-documented suspicion and mistrust of relief personnel. Africa, long considered by the west to be a primal and underdeveloped wasteland, has matured quite a bit in recent decades and has flourishing cities and highways to show for it. However, it's those same highways that are allowing West Africans to travel freely and to spread more rapidly an already easily contracted virus. West Africa is also largely comprised of animist whose beliefs in regard to the handling of the dead (*they believe that the dead should be washed and prepared for burial*) make the disease hard to contain. It's not hard to imagine how westerners and long time ravishers of African countries, who came this time with hazmat suits, body bags and large white tents (that no one ever comes out of alive), could cause a rift in trust. This mistrust makes the disease hard to treat and contain and it makes it hard for relief personnel to educate and interact with natives without being attacked and chased away.

I was back in the driver's seat of my car now, no longer speeding, no longer weaving. I couldn't help but try to think of a solution to the problem. I struggled because I'm not a doctor and I'm far from an expert and even if I was there is no cure for irony. Here I was on a highway that brought life and business and freedom and ease of access; on the other side of the ocean exists a highway just like this one spreading one of the deadliest diseases known to man. Simultaneously, this same country that was being done in by an advanced infrastructure was also being eaten alive by an ancient animist tradition and a deep-seated mistrust of westerners. The irony involved in being ravaged by the future and the past is incurable.

As I pulled into the parking lot at work I closed my eyes briefly and asked for clarity. There was so much information to take in and so many variables to consider and yet I was sure that there was a solution. I opened my eyes just as the Sun began to shine, waking the clouds and confirming the conclusion I had just arrived at. There was a light behind the fog of our everyday routines and ideologies. After all, Ebola is not the only disease for which there is no immediate cure; it is rivaled by AIDS/HIV, cancer, war, hate, envy, greed and the list goes on. If there were a point to it all, I'd wager that it doesn't begin and end with curing the diseases themselves but with treating our interactions and relationships and our notions and ideas. Perhaps this isn't really about finding cures at all; perhaps it's about finding communion.

Misunderstanding is the most widely contracted disease for which everyone has a cure. Irony.

Hem

the took

don't usually know there's no touching
without taking - the hopes and turmoil and
energy and affinity

without sharing (on purpose or residually)

or maybe they do know and they don't
care or can't measure what they've given,
what they've gotten

or can't remember or won't remember the
love leaving them when they were touched

I remember...when she hugged me she
grabbed my back and tried to pull herself
through me...strained herself to strain
herself and leave me with all those
demons...I've been took and I've taken and
I can't blame her...we all need saving...if
there is a God then one day I'll be walking
in a crowd and anxiously bump my savior
and she'll turn and she'll ask "who touched
me?"

Austin Vandorian Grier

From On The Mountain 2

The word as it has been given to me from where I received it.

~~~

The Light

1 The world of mortal men is shrouded in a persistent darkness and blessed are those who clamor for the light,

2 And blessed are those who reject the darkness because where there is ignorance, violence and greed and cruelty run like rivers

3 There is much that man does not know and there is much more that man will never know

4 What has been revealed to him is that with which he can do good works

5 The attention a man lends is the light of his world

and everything exposed to that light grows.

[6] His consideration is considerable because his deliberation makes the world fertile.

[7] His thoughts and intentions are loyal to their creator and they dig in, planting roots and sowing seeds until the childish foliage of his imagination becomes the mature forest of his reality.

[8] His concentration makes the vastness of doubt a stones-throw and his observation impregnates opportunity, swelling it with possibility.

[9] It is for this reason that he is careful not to build monuments in the image of his misery or alters in the likeness of his abrasions.

[10] He is slow to bathe in pity and even slower to wallow in shame because he knows that his attention is an amplifying multiplier.

[11] He knows that he is an agent of augmentation so he is careful.

Austin Vandorian Grier

[12] When a man shows care and is deliberate with his attention he allows himself to become a vessel for the one who carved him from muddy ignorance and he transforms himself from a raging and destructive flame to a beacon of hope and faith and good work.

Kingdom Come

Thy kingdom come, Thy will be done in earth, as it is in heaven.

Matthew 6: 10

~~~

I remember leaving the warmth emanating from the bordered mosaic brick walkway that ran down from Martin Luther King Jr Drive, pouting and dragging into the cold and sterile hallways of the W.B. Atkinson building on my way to biology class. I dreaded the class because the information felt elementary at best and my classmates regarded the work as if it was rocket science and my professor approached the subject as if it was in an adult magazine and I was caught in the middle.

I didn't dislike biology but I fostered a heavy disdain for all that is trivial and any class requiring only memorization and regurgitation would immediately pirouette its way onto my shit list. I had very little patience for things that didn't challenge me or allow me to be imaginative. There was a stench like death that clung to postulations and theories that were widely accepted and hardly challenged and my attention span ran wild whenever I got a whiff of any putative school of thought. I rewarded my professor for his time and expertise by sitting in the middle of the third row which all of the education experts I had ever encountered affectionately referred to as part of *the T*, a sacred area that supposedly led professors to believe that any student seated there was serious about education. I rewarded myself for taking the initiative of attending biology by taking naps during the class.

My disinterest persisted through cell structure, cellular processes and biological phylum. It wasn't until we arrived at Darwinism that my interest peaked. Notions of natural selection intrigued me and I became a fan of the school of thought, though unconvinced of its validity. I enjoyed our discussion, albeit brief, of natural selection as a replacement for creation stories and religious dogma. There were those who favored religion and argued that life (man specifically) was far too advanced for atmosperic accidents to have been his origin and the existence of what they perceived as a soul and purpose and heaven and hell wouldn't allow them to accept this theory. Then there were those who did not believe in God and did not credit the existence of man to Adam and Eve or Father Sky and Mother Earth. They found little comfort in myths defined by ex nihilo creation stories and instead found confidence in measurable phenomena.

I found myself in the middle. I couldn't see why natural selection couldn't be an instrument of God. I argued that man is born in a measly and unimpressive state and yet he evolves and changes and adapts, and when he has reached maturity he is almost a different being altogether. In the same way all of creation is one being created by a superior God who allowed his infantile and unimpressive creation to evolve through natural selection over thousands of years until we had become advanced enough to discredit him. My theories were not met well on either side of the issue and though I was entertained by the exchange I felt strangely alone. I recall trying to brush off whatever effect the discussion had on me but initially I failed. I didn't know what was bothering me or why but I knew that something about the discourse and that subject was supposed to mean something to me. It was supposed to matter. At the time I couldn't fathom what that purpose might be so I went back to my dorm and wrote out my thoughts in a notebook that I wouldn't see again until years later. I entitled the entry The Kingdom of God.

~~~

I found my notebook in my parent's home six years later, one week after white police officers shot an unarmed Walter Scott in the back and planted a gun on him. I was confused about what I had been feeling with regard to the news and I went diving for my old notebooks as a result. Whenever I was lacking inspiration or clarity I consulted with my younger self. He seemed much more certain about the world he lived in. He didn't waste time on syntax and mechanisms. His writings were raw, premature, nutritious and slimy, I could always submerge myself in them and they coated and fed me like embryotic fluid. I couldn't place my feelings and at the point when my accuracy was its highest (and yet and still very poor) I decided that the best way to describe it was a reeling sensation. I felt as though there was something I knew or something that I was feeling that I had never experienced before or that I didn't have the words to articulate. It was much like when you run a fever and nothing hurts and you can't describe your discomfort, you know only that you are uncomfortable. I went diving to see if I might come across some confession that might resonate with me. Hours passed and I had just put down a yellow seventy-page notebook when I saw a dusty spine bound lab book. I flipped through it not expecting to find anything but restlessness made me thumb through to the end and I found these words tucked there:

I have seen God many times and did not know him. I know this to be true because I have dodged mirrors and other people. I have not helped when I could have helped and I have not lifted myself from the depths because I was waiting for someone else to come and lift me. All along I have been what I sought because my creator made me apart from him and yet he is a part of me. When man was tasked with describing and naming the smallest thing that can exist while still carrying the properties of a thing he spoke and said atom. When God was tasked with creating the smallest thing that can exist and retain the properties of a thing he spoke and created the kingdom of god. He wrote it on the wall of the membranes of our cells and his handwriting is so small that modern man has not developed eyes that can see it or a language that will allow him to read it. However, man can feel it rising in himself. When he is a baby and has never eaten and has never seen a nipple he knows to suckle. His cells have no mind of their own and yet they excrete and produce in a fashion that allows them to live. The writing on the wall tells man that he has a future and plight and the capacity to love and to aspire. Unlike the rest of creation man is not destined only to survive as animals survive. He has been afforded the opportunity to thrive. Man and man's cells seek equilibrium and stasis and they move and produce and excrete in a way that allows them to achieve what they desire. Man can also learn. He can find that there are many ways to achieve his aspirations. He can find that murder and theft and greed and lies can get him what he wants. He can find that there is such a thing as righteousness and he can choose to follow it. He will feel the urge to be righteous and to thrive and expand and grow and learn. His evolution will be facilitated by his survival and his willingness to go further and to build. When his livelihood and righteousness are threatened man will writhe in pain as the kingdom of god rises inside of him and rights him. It is this impulse that makes a drowning man open his mouth when he knows there is no air. It is the need to remain alive so that you can build even in the face of the abyss. Such is the writing on the wall, the semipermeable membrane and such is the kingdom of God, the essence of man and the substance of his spirit.

I set the book in my lap after reading the passage four or five times. There are moments when we come to ourselves, as if our bodies call out to us after astral projection. I felt gravity grab at my consciousness and I was dragged down into a sea of things I had always known that were hidden from me. The disquiet that I had been feeling was a ripple through creation that shook those with a conscience. There's an overbearing insensitivity to pain and turmoil in this world that is a direct result of smothering the kingdom inside of you. Years of attempting to care and feel less had developed as a warped survival tool fashioned to help me survive. If I'm dead they can't kill me. If I'm hurt then they can't hurt me. If I don't love anyone or anything then they can't take anything from me.

I remember seeing the ticker crawl across the screen detailing the shooting of Walter Scott. I wasn't heartbroken then, nor was I bothered outside of the quiet disdain that comes from knowing better; If my heart were broken every time a white cop acted out his intimate executioner fantasies I would never know love. All of those emotions came to me at once and I was transported instantaneously to the dark cave of vulnerability. I realized and accepted all at once that my life was not my own and my fears and worries and concerns were not my own. These things had been crafted for me and fitted for me and attached to me like weighted shackles. I felt afraid and sad and depressed and defeated. I can't go outside for fear of being killed or framed or judged or feared or profiled or marginalized or hated or ridiculed. My experience is and has been rooted in surviving and not in thriving. I was up to my chest in sorrow when I felt it rising in me. I felt the sunrise on my face in a dark place. I was not created to crawl on my belly or to cower at the feet of men. I imagine this is the feeling that the Afrocentric lecturers wish us to feel when they speak ceaselessly of Africa, the overwhelming pride and joy that comes from knowing that you have been supplied with a kingdom for you to build. It surged up through my chest, the urge to exert myself and my life and my talent. I reflected on those who had gotten us this far and I found that they had always come in times of universal darkness, when the world and space they occupied was overcast with oppression and violence. I know that must have weighed down on them and caused their shoulders and spirits to droop. I thought of Amiri and Booker of Langston and Richard. I know this is how we made it this far.

The inclination has always been there, jammed tigerishly between remnants of who we were and evidence of who we are, a silent and gentle urge that crawls from one synapses to another. I think that maybe we have always felt it. Perhaps we didn't understand what we were feeling until we saw flowers planted in the shade lean toward the Sun. I've thought often since then, maybe it's possible that we took Rosa's defiance for frustration,

Austin Vandorian Grier

Malcolm's heat for anger, King's dream for a sermon; maybe we failed to acknowledge what really bubbled up inside of them. Perhaps we failed to acknowledge that what we witnessed wasn't the random reactions of persecuted people backed into a corner. Perhaps it was more than that; maybe it was the blueprint of a better life that welled up inside of them almost bursting them at the seams. It bubbled up and rolled out of Rosa's mouth and she said, "I am tired." She wasn't talking about her feet; she was talking about the fatigue that comes from suppressing your creator's designs and accepting a life of servitude. It bubbled up inside of Martin and rolled out of his mouth and he said, "We've got some difficult days ahead, but it really doesn't matter with me know because I've been to the mountaintop." His eyes were full of tears and I know he saw what I saw after I closed that book and sank to the floor. I saw all the little black faces I had ever seen basking in the Sun and I knew no fear and I knew no shame and I knew no reservation, nor malice, nor greed, nor jealously. I knew only love and hope. I knew that deep in my cells God had drawn plans for me on the walls of my existence with melanin.

I knew then like I know now that the kingdom isn't behind us, nor is it above us, and the kingdom will not lower itself from the Heavens, it will come from within and it will be built...by us and for us.

Austin Vandorian Grier

Saturn

I rode a black bullet through the city with
you, there was aggressive signage and an
electric breeze and the streetlights were
on fire burning in amber and honeydew

I watched the world bend to your gravity,
all the air dragged by your hair and the
lights drew to you and then the music and
then me

the world orbited you on a black bullet and
I was content as a ring and a witness

Around The Corner

there's a home for me at the nape of your
neck, next to a roundabout where there's
always traffic

we would fit together like Lincoln blocks
and form something just as nostalgic; we
were even a rubix cube once

I remember falling asleep in your hand and
your heartbeat woke me up, I was almost
home in my dream and you were too

Austin Vandorian Grier

Kink

a few times I couldn't tell our limbs apart
and what I was feeling was a feral four
legged emotion tangled like we were and
we were a Bachmann knot coiled and
recoiled

we were drifting debris briefly and when it
was time to head back I reached out to
touch your face and felt my hand on my
cheek, after I understood how – we went
home

From On The Mountain 3

The word as it has been given to me from where I received it.

~~~

The Humble Capstone

1 I beseech you therefore, brethren, humble yourselves and know that your gifts are not your own. ² A foolish man exalts himself in the presence of God and when is man not in the presence of God? ³ Who has raised you from the dead? Who has carved you from the mud? Who among you has birthed himself? Who among you has saved himself from himself?

⁴ Man's time has been gifted to him and he cannot touch the four corners of the earth at once and yet he exalts himself. ⁵ The meek shall inherit the world and yet man's pride is mighty. ⁶ When he is met with good fortune he is also God, having birthed and erected himself.

[7] When he is met with poor fortune he curses God. [8] He turns his back on the light and whimpers in the dark. [9] He meditates to himself while wallowing in his pain and his meditations bore holes in his spirit. He whispers to himself.

[10] I do not worship a merciful God. I have been sought out by Satan and I do not serve a God who would protect me. [11] I have been righteous. [12] I have been upright. I have given to the beggars at the beautiful gate. [13] I have not coveted. I do not steal. I do not lie. I have not killed. I am above reproach. [14] I have made myself a great and honest man.
[15] The Lord mocks me. Perhaps he does not see me. I am good.

[16] I tell you the truth; man in all of his fearful wonder has never been above suffering.
[17] Who among you knows compassion but has not known loss? [18] When man is suffering he looks to the sky for relief. [19] He pleads with his maker to show him the way. [20] He busies himself with the moon and the stars and signs and constellations. [21] While his neck is craned and his eyes are strained he fails to see that the path to

his salvation has been lit by his agony and his loss and his anguish.

22 Man is a seaman whose oceans heave and rage and bark and swell in the dark of night until the sea and the sky are one and man believes that he will surely die. 23 He lays prostate and asks the lord to calm the waves and he is blinded by desperation and his eyes become cloudy and he cannot see that great storms craft great navigators and have you not been directed to navigate?

24 The great navigator has to have been where he is navigating. He has trekked through many valleys and scaled many mountains. 25 He has taken wrong turns and has been overcome with despair. 26 He has had to find his hope and then he has had to find his way. 27 He has made it back to where he started and so he knows the way. 28 He has been blessed with an overflowing fountain that gushes and runs over with experience and he drinks from it when there is famine where there should be faith. 29He has ventured into the darkness so that he can see the light.

30 It is hard for man to see God when he has never seen the abyss. 31 It is hard for

man to discern light from light and good from good and surviving from thriving and so he is led into the darkness that he may see the world as his maker would have him to see it. [32] He is vetted in the darkness and he is charged with shining his light and he is no longer afraid of struggle and pain and agony; he welcomes all with which he can do good works.

[33] Man in all of his fearful wonder is the crown of creation in the holy tapestry and even at his peak he is still below his maker. [34] His maker is light. [35] Good health, good fortune, wine, stables and fine clothes shining brightly can only distort vision and man when draped in these riches shines brightly and it becomes hard for man to know light from light and so a net of darkness is cast so that man can discern his maker from his earthly spoils and his purpose from his pleasures and then, and only then, is man equipped to take the world and its people on his shoulders that he may be humbled and lead all that linger in the dark into the light.

Starbucks' Race Together

The Apotheosis of Illness

"YOUR WORD IS YOUR BOND! Do you understand that? Can you feel that when I say it to you? That sums up everything I've told you so far. You really aren't going to understand shit that I'm trying to get through to you until you understand that. YOUR WORD IS YOUR BOND! That's big with us yaknow?

Yeah yeah I'm going to explain, think about it this way, eons ago when man was an unintelligent hunchback he ran into other unintelligent hunchbacks and they figured out how to communicate with each other. They probably started out with mad grunts and bogus ass hand signals but they got the job done. They probably moved on to figuring out how to collectively feed themselves and after that they no doubt figured out that they had more than they could eat all at once. They looked around and had extra meat and tools and now they had assets. Next, they figure how to barter and when that becomes inefficient they create currency and learn to steal. That's the natural

progression of things and then there's us.
Our origin was void of that natural
progression yaknow?

We were herded over here and placed
purposely with people who spoke a
different language so we couldn't
communicate. We were denied language
and assets and opportunity but humans
won't go without that for long. We learned
English and we formed bonds that
transcend family and tribe and though we
didn't have many assets or any money we
facilitated our transactions with our word
and our word was just as good as your
money. Probably better because it can't
be inflated. And here we are at the root of
what it is I'm describing to you. My distrust
comes from your inability to do what you
said you would do. How can I respect you
after that? How can we work together?
How can we live together without you
addressing it?

Yes, you! You don't feel responsible and I
can see that on your face. What? What is
it? You want to tell me that you weren't
there right? You probably want me to say
that you're absolved because there's
nothing you can do about what happened
four hundred years ago but I won't say

that. I won't ever fix my mouth to say that shit! I won't ever fix my mouth to say that because you aren't different than they are. You all haven't kept your word since you started this country and that's the root of the distrust. Your word is your bond and your bank and your people are bankrupt. No value. No equity. Nothing! This is what I know to be true, there is no population on the face of this planet that has come in contact with you that you haven't attempted to ravish or rape or eliminate or all the above. What's worse is that you want to skim over it, in school and in conversation. Right now you're uncomfortable talking about something that you say you had nothing to do with and do you know why that is?

It's because your spirit isn't going to entertain that bullshit either. You didn't lift a hand to oppress me and at first glance that's fair if the analysis stops there but I'm not so dull. You live and thrive from a privilege that treachery has afforded you. At any point you can choose to cash in on your skin color and whether you choose to acknowledge that or not every time you do so, you do it at the expense of me.

I know you aren't going to own that, I knew that before I said it. That really just brings us back to where we started. There has to be a reckoning, there has to be an apology, and there has to be reparation. I asked you for what I deserved and you put a snake in my hand. I asked you for reparation and you gave me welfare. So yes, I am sick but I am not the sickness. I'm a symptom and how could I not be? How could this play out any differently? Answer me dammit, don't just sit there with that look in your eyes because it's telling and it's irritating. It says that no matter how hard you try you can't understand and you can't understand because you can't empathize and you can't empathize without condemning yourself. It would seem that spiritually your position is as bad as mine. And yet, I believe you're better off because you have the capacity to get better and to evolve incessantly. No roadblocks. No speed bumps. No gerrymandering. No redlining. No lynching. No wanton murders. Nothing can stop you from deciding that you want to improve your state, spiritually or physically. Not one damn thing.

Me? Ha! ME! Nothing can stop me? Have I offended you? If so, I apologize but I must have offended you for you to jest at such a sore spot. Did you mean that? Yaknow...what you said, did you mean it?

I see.

Let me ask you a question. Pull up closer I'm not going to bite you, I just want you to really hear this.

What happens to a person if you keep them in perpetual darkness for a long period of time?

Good answer but nah, I think that permanent blindness is a myth. There is a period of impaired vision though so remember you said that.

While in the darkness people experience extreme paranoia, restlessness, and time slows for them. Their wake/sleep cycles slip into rotations of thirty-six hours active and twelve hours resting. When they are released from the darkness they experience an impaired ability to process information, a reduction in memory functions and increases in suggestibility. What does that mean to you?

Yes...ok, but why do you think I would ask you something like that here?

Shit...look, ok, I apologize for cursing...my intention isn't to be cryptic I just want you to take part in your emancipation by thinking.

Close, I asked you that because this country, not just my people or yours, but the entire country has been shrouded in perpetual darkness since 1617. I'll give you a moment to deal with that.

The darkness in this particular case is ignorance and arrogance and greed and evil and malice, you follow?

We've been on this journey in darkness together since the beginning, with varying results, but we've been together nonetheless. While in this darkness time has slowed and allowed you to believe that slavery and it's offspring didn't last that long. Perhaps even that you have outlived them. For me it makes me feel as if it were so long ago or as if the days under the whip might have been shorter than my hour here with you. You have become increasingly paranoid, believing that one-day we may rise up and enslave you, maybe even taking your daughters for our wives and your wives as our cattle.

I didn't interrupt you please do not interrupt me.

Your paranoia is misplaced because only one race has proved willing and capable of doing such things. For me it has led me to believe that everything that exists, especially the people who look like me, are here to do me harm or disservice. It leads me to believe that I am in this place alone. Who can I trust?

On the rare occasion that light shines on us, like when the Freedmen's Schools opened or when Rustin set in motion what would be the SCLC or when Brooks wrote We Real Cool, we collectively were blind to the redemption, the prophets and the warnings. With you, it became hard to process information like why we have so many fathers missing after your welfare required that no father be in the home…or, like when you all did studies about the STD rates in my community but left out how you did and still do wide spread STD experimentation in our neighborhoods. For us, it was hard to calculate, without a formal education, the damage that had been done to us. There are people who have suffered far less than us who suffer from PTSD and few who have suffered more than we and yet we can't count high enough to count the trespasses.

For you, having spent so much time in the dark, it was hard for you to remember what you did to me, so much so that you can't even recall how what was done back then may affect what you have going on right now. For me, it allowed me to forget what you did to me. Perhaps that was another life and another time and not something that I should waste my time on, after all you weren't actually there and neither was I, correct?

With you, it allowed your elders to suggest to you that manifest destiny had some sort of merit. They taught you that here in America every man has the capacity to pull himself by his own bootstraps and to chart his own course...maybe, even go as far as to chart his own destiny. What a load of shit that was. Your forefathers told you that and didn't even live that way themselves. Initially, their gardens where seeded by natives and their homes built by the indentured and their America was built by me. With me, it compelled my father to suggest to me that if I were to play nice, pull my pants up, stop wearing long shirts, don't whistle, don't talk to white women, don't touch anything in the store, don't look cops in the eye, don't reach for my wallet, don't get arrested, don't fail at doing twice as good for half as much…that maybe we would be ok. What a load of shit that was. What a load of Uncle Tom shit that was! It won't be ok because I can go to school my entire life and study hard and play the game straight and become a professor at Harvard and be arrested for entering my own home. I could venture out to get a snack and be hunted down by some murderous mall cop and murdered in the street, couldn't I?

Look around, yes…right now. You see how no one is looking at us? That's a natural response when people like me seem angry. They probably want to know what's got me so upset. I probably have babymomma drama. Ha! They probably think I need a hug and some love and it'll all get better. I think that's an interesting thought, yaknow…love as a cure for all of this.

You ever watched Mad Men?

No?

It's a show about this advertising firm and this ad guy, Draper. Draper's real cool, yaknow one of those pseudo-deep cynical types that pulls a cigarette at just the right moment to get the lady's blood flowing, it's a cool move, yaknow the cigarette thing, I admit it. Anyway, on this one particular episode Draper is in his office with one of those "I need a cool, cigarette-smoking ad guy to get my blood flowing" type and they're discussing love. After taking a long hit of one of his cigarettes Draper remarks to the girl that love was something ad men created to sell hosiery. I believe that. I believe that men like Draper and guys who look like you created love as we understand it and that's why it won't work as a cure. Would you believe that the people who taught me what love is also let slaves vote before their women? Pretty wild huh?

I can see why you might say that but that's not my point. The point is that love isn't universal. Sure, there's love everywhere and everyone wants it but its meaning and application aren't universal. That's why I think love, as a cure for all of this is interesting. I was brought up under your definition, which I've recently cast off but had I kept it I wouldn't be able to have this conversation. It's all a logical thing really. Love directed outward has to start within the person dispensing or demonstrating it, if for no other reason than origin and trajectory saying that's where it came from. The love that you have for yourself and your so-called manifest destiny is rooted in self-edification and imperialism and it requires that you view everything and everyone as things to be consumed.

Naturally, you disagree but I'm pulling you from the darkness so I don't expect you to see it right away.

And before you accuse me of it again, no I am not being condescending.

This is why we always hear these back-to-the-motherland lectures from my side. For those who don't mean physically going back, what they are alluding to are the concepts we employed back then. Love that is rooted in community and not self or things or status yaknow?

Ha! That's an interesting thing to hear coming from you.

Are you trolling me or you really want answer?

Ok, let's see.

First, I think that it's pretty ironic that you would advise me against making broad and sweeping determinations with regard to race considering it was broad and sweeping determinations based on race that got me to this country in the first place. It was those same broad and sweeping determinations that kept Jim Crow and "separate but equal" in play for so long that they are still a part of our infrastructure and it is in fact those same broad and sweeping determinations that just yesterday led a officer on UNCG's campus to tweet out a crime alert warning students to be on the lookout for a black male with big lips.

Secondly, I think it's impossible for people like me to be racist because racism means something different in this country. It's not just feelings of disdain or superiority based on race it's institutional. It's built into our prisons, schools, courts, cops, hospitals, doctors, politics and religions. We cannot be racist because we did not create these things and we are not in control of them now.

That is a good point; we do bring a few of these things on ourselves but how else could this play out?

Maybe I should explain it this way. We were a people with an identity and we had that identity stolen from us. Our experience in this country since that robbery has been one of pain and violence and struggle and self-loathing and loss and illness. People need identity to survive and so we cling to the experiences that we have and try our best to do right by those experiences, sometimes even subconsciously and sometimes to our own demise. Which is why being a real nigga never involves anything good. It's always something violent or involving pain and struggle and loss. That's how real is defined because that's how real life has been for those people. That's why the youth gravitate toward hyperbole when they express themselves and normal puberty-induced mood swings become self-diagnosed bipolar disorder. They don't know that isn't who they are and they have raised that sickness to God level.

However, their condition is not their fault, no, that fault lies with you and I.

Which is why I need to get going, I have a class to teach and a part to play in setting them free. As do you!

No, no I wouldn't expect you to agree after only an hour…it took us centuries to get free and we still have to have this conversation but your endurance gives me hope.

No, of course!

You as well sir, Godspeed!"

Guerilla

there's a war going on outside, no man is
safe from...that advertisements hover over
Time Square...to keep us safe from

contemporary man says that early man
collected ammo in the form of a berry and
stuffed a banana clip in the form of a
mouth to spray like a flamethrower...color
all over the walls of a place...homo erectus
though not complex erected a connection
between his chromatic Desert Eagle and
cold stone walls turned easels

man's most natural inclination is to control
his space...poor soul probably looked
around his cave...sighed...thought about
his day

grunting bitch woman
bad hunt
and had to turn in early for the sleepy sun

and he sprayed
1969
Cornbread wanders out into the streets in
Philly
with an AK 47 paint can

Austin Vandorian Grier

he cranes his neck and looks around his
cave
and he sprays

he figures you are marking changing
spraying

or

you're being marked changed sprayed

man declares war on his surroundings
says to them I want you to reflect me
a little more than I reflect you
a battle waged and war is fought
over who reflects who
and so he aspires to be a little less Stoop
Kid...a little more Basquiat
drew a paint brush donning a crown of
thorns on his desk as a warning shot

illicit urban intervention by typographic
terrorist believers in pure public space
quintessential spatial Marxist

they run rampant in the city cover
everything with color to save the soul old
and broken who would dare call colors
ugly...they drape the walls with heavy
illustrations

praying that they will buckle and
give...artistic Malthusians...something has
to die so we can live

and so they kill the bridges walls and halls
that attempt to hold us down and hold us
in...spraying

cultural appropriation dollars frown down
on them...they'd pay to have them moved

because as long as they are bombing
walls
who's reflecting who?

The Deacon's Prayer, An Inadvertent Sermon

Good Morning Brothers and Sisters!

Awwh that was weak! I said GOOD MORNING BROTHERS AND SISTERS!

Much better, ain't no need in us inviting the Holy Spirit into this place if we're going to be dead when it gets here. Amen!

Now I have to say I wouldn't have had to say good morning a second time if I had started out with 3 IN THE MORNING AT THE PANCAKE HOUSE!

I know ya'll didn't know I knew anything about that but what a shame it would be to find out that you would raise your voice out there and sit meek in here. Amen!

Amen!

I know some of you are still tired from last night but the Lord has saw fit to bring you to this appointed place at this appointed time and your legs carried you and you are in your right mind so lets give God some praise! Amen!

I don't know what it is that brought you to this church house this morning. It may have been sickness that is making your body weak, perhaps you have come for healing and I am here to tell you that you have come to the right place! Maybe you came because your spirit has been low and downtrodden and you needed to hear a word of praise to lift you for the slump you're in. I came to tell you that you have come to the right place! Maybe you have come seeking understanding because the world has you all confused and conflicted and my God! I have come to tell you that you have come to the right place. You know the word of God says that in all things God works for the good of those love him, who have been called according to his purpose. So you have come to the right place this morning!

What a beautiful day it is in the house of the Lord. I am overjoyed to see you all this morning and oh how beautiful you all look, thank God for that church!

Thank God for Sister Williams this morning! PRAISE THE LORD! Sister Williams I almost didn't see you sitting over there in the glare, Lord I could hardly tell you apart from the light, you look so good! Did we not JUST pray a season ago that the season of sickness would leave Sister Williams and here she is in the pew looking even better than I!

As I scan the pews once more I see Brother Harris Burgundy, Trustee Burgundy's grandson, is back from overseas. His body and his mind are whole praise God church! Did we not pray for the safe return of Brother Burgundy? Praise him from whom all blessings flow hallelujah!

You all look so beautiful this morning. You look like flowers blooming in here and the sun is streaming and it's shining on you and you look like you may have a testimony this morning! You know church there were people who didn't praise and didn't pray and had plans of getting up this morning and did not, come on church! I want my God to find me ready!

You know church, you got up this morning and I hope the beautiful words of exaltation were on your tongue before your feet hit the floor. I came here this morning church to let you know that there is a God who sits high and looks low.

If you all would stand together in the presence of God, every head bowed and every eye closed, as we invite the Holy Spirit into this place.

Shall we pray together?

God of Abraham, Isaac and Jacob, Miriam, Debra, and Ester...thou who art my creator, my redeemer and sustainer...thou who art from everlasting to everlasting.

Today we come to you in humble subjugation having found that we are nothing without your mercy, grace and favor. Lord we find strength in knowing that we even when we plan that you guide our steps and clear the path. We know that your word says that you are our refuge and our strength and an ever-present help in our time of need. We need you this morning father!

We have tried our way Lord. We have ventured out far and wide with the gifts and talents you have given us. We have enjoyed a life of riches beyond what we deserve. We have looked into the mirror in the morning and thought to ourselves that we are the source of our good fortune. We have gone to work without you father.

Austin Vandorian Grier

We have gone into marriage without you
father. We have gone into battle in the
streets for our rights without you father.
We have come into church without you
father and we don't want to be without you
any longer.

Our well has run dry and we have found
that we are not the source of all things that
are good and holy, no father, we know
now and confess that we are only vessels
and agents of our creator. We know that
you put us here for a specific and
necessary work and we know that our
temple is temporary and our time is limited
and the work created for us to do will go
undone if we don't do it. We have faith
that you will guide our steps as you see fit
because your word says faith is
confidence in what we hope for and
assurance about what we do not see and
we wish for nothing more than to be a light
on a hill.

Lord we know that you have plans for us,
plans to prosper us and not to harm us,
plans to give us hope and a future. Lord
this world and our people have known a
great suffering and have witnessed a great
evil. Lord, suit us in your armor and make
us warriors for justice and for peace,

prosperity and charity. We don't just want to take up space Father God!

Lord we ask that you give us the thoughts to think and the words to say and plans to execute so that we may be a pivotal instrument in exercising your will. We ask that you sharpen us that we may be on the cutting edge of the age of peace and prosperity that you promised us. We ask that you hang us on that polished wheel that we may be reshaped in your image as creators.

Father God we ask that you give us the courage to do what is difficult and the courage to do what is right. We have been held low by this world and it's institutions. Money and drugs and sex and visions of grandeur have distracted us but we ask Father that you grant us sobriety that we may be able to see and think clearly. We ask that your spark in our mind memories of where we have come from and how we came to be here so that we might know what we are capable of, for we are fearfully and wonderfully made. We ask that you erect in us a healthy pride in our heritage and our roots because your word says that: at least there is hope for a tree, if it is cut down, it will sprout again, and its new shoots will not fail. Its roots may grow old in the ground and its stump die in the soil, yet at the scent of water it will bud and put forth shoots like a plant. Help us to put forth shoots Lord!

Raise our spirits and countenance so much so that we can join in with the choir and bless your manservant who will stand behind this sacred desk, lower him into the well of wisdom that he might overflow and then tip him over so that he may flow like a great fountain, that your word may run like a river and permeate and saturate our souls.

We ask that you guide the direction of the service that it may go wherever you would have it to go.

All of these things we ask in the name of the Father, the Son and the Holy Ghost.

Amen!

From On The Mountain 4

The word as it has been given to me from where I received it

~~~

The Mason and The Prophet

1 And then a mason spoke saying, but Master, we have left our old homes and departed from our old ways and have settled here in newness and righteousness, how can this place be no better than where we have traveled from?

2 And he answered saying, man may feel a fire set in his soul and under his feet and when compelled by conviction he will travel far and wide like seeds in the wind. 3 He will build where he has come from and he will recreate home wherever he goes. 4 And though his convictions are strong and his intentions are good man will rebuild where he has come from even if in his building he crafts his own demise.

5 And to this the mason replied saying, but master we once lived on barren and flat

land and now we have come to rocky
shores and rolling hills, surely this place is
nothing like where we have come from.

[6] And he answered saying, man will
venture out into the world and recreate
where he has come from but man does not
come from a place on a map and hands
and mortar cannot erect his home. [7] No,
home is where man's mind goes when he
closes his eyes. [8] His home is the city of
his soul.

[9] It is because man is an augmenter and
creator that he excels at bringing the city
of his soul to fruition and so before setting
out he must build a suitable place for
himself in his soul because he will rebuild
this city for himself daily.

[10] If a man has a prison in the city of his
soul he will build a prison for himself and
subject himself to it or he will subject
himself to the prisons of others. [11] Thus
man must keep the designs of prosperity,
community, race pride, generosity,
compassion, faith, gravity, creativity and
enlightenment at the center of his soul.

[12] Man must keep his heart and his mind
because they together are the seat of the

city of his soul. [13] Whatsoever enters the mind or heart of a man becomes a part of his design. [14] Those things allowed to enter the seat become a man's design and they are the things he will eventually build or refuse to destroy.

[15] Man will fail to destroy that which exists outside of himself if it mirrors what is in him even if his failure means certain death because it is suicide to kill even a part of himself. [16] In order for man to eliminate what surrounds him, he must first search the seat of the city of his soul and find that which he seeks to destroy does not reside there. [17] If he is host to such foul things he must isolate and remove them through the meditations of his heart and the conditioning of his mind.

[18] A man with poverty residing in the city of his soul naturally has poverty in his heart and on his mind. [20] He will build slums everywhere that he goes or he will subject himself to slums and he will be unable to cure the world of slums or remove himself from slums until he has successfully eradicated the slums in the city of his soul.

Austin Vandorian Grier

Lava

your skin is so hot

we tumble into bed and a cold night cant
touch me but in the morning I cant reach a
cool breeze

If I could I'd trace all of your smoldering
features but id lose all of my
distinguishable features

I wonder if I could keep you and remain
myself

I'm a fire blanket and dry wood and
gasoline

I wasn't before but I am now

Lighting Rod

love and hate are both slate blue
they tell me what's important is what things
have in common

but

I'm not certain I buy that sermon

but

there's no doubt that all of your feelings
burn the air in the room

and me

I always burn and smolder and glow like
Samson's irons

and

I have to because I am all that has
withstood you

and

I'll allow you to melt me to save us

Austin Vandorian Grier

Exceedingly

to get where we're going we'll have to take
it too far

previously

I've crossed lines but not my T's –
neglected a few I's

with you, I push forward – sometimes I hit
your heart, most times your

kidneys

every time, I hit something

I wonder where you go after having gone
too far

probably the same place not going far
enough takes you

love is hitting a pinhead with a cannon

I wonder how I could love you without
crushing you, probably can't

Mercurial

I dangled off a cliff once in a cave made of
her, grasping for life and limb from a limb –
flailing

I was looking for her in a cave made of
her, I leaned on a false wall and it gave
way to her but I didn't find her, I found
favor

I'm not sure that I earned it but I kept it and
kept going, I pressed forward and leaned
over the railing

I peeked down into the pit where I couldn't
see the black in the abyss and I was
squinting down when an earthquake sent
me sailing

Austin Vandorian Grier

Diving

I heard her speak and her mouth was a
geyser in the middle of a king desert that
could not be confused with some minor
cooler desert

and

words ran over her lips like a herd clinging
together for life, each word was dependent
on the one before it and the one after it

and

when it seemed that her words had
traveled far enough and would finally
reach me the heat peaked and they turned
to steam and there was a cloud between
her and I

and

I knew that this was the tip of her ice burg
and so I teased the waters edge looking
but not moving, searching for the rest of
her in my reflection on the face of the
water as if time would reveal her for me
and when time was not enough I decided

I'd had enough of waiting and I dived in and swam to the bottom of the sea and was crushed by her ocean.

Austin Vandorian Grier

Continuum

from where I'm sitting I think I can reach
out and twist off a corner of you for
myself, the margin for close and far is the
same

I think I could live with barely transcending
space and time and perhaps cutting it as
close as the skin on my teeth if I could
reach you, right now – on a good day, at
best, I'm a good memory – next lifetime I
wont let you leave

Native Tongue

for Shevy

ah she always had words for me

ah eke tu nu jonu pawol pu me

words like sweet corn and yams and
molasses

me ah du me and yams molasses

except when we met.. no, when we met
there weren't any words

le lujaun.. no, ley nu jan pa ne pes pawol

there was no silence and no words but i
heard her over the noise

*pa te ne pes silence ek pa te ne pes pawol, me
pa pale but me tan dezod la*

her head was tilted downward and her
sunglasses were pushed up high on her
nose

*tet le te desan epe sunglasses la te mu te a le
ney*

Austin Vandorian Grier

I couldn't see those almond eyes but I'm
certain they were closed

me pa te sa we zey but mey te le de zey te fame

her lips were parted slightly, they were so
full

leve le te ovwe , ey te ple

they had a pleasant swell to them, filled
with a sweet remorse.. like they wished
they had said things they would never say

*ey te a fley, te le abo remorse, me ka quey me ka
di ahbagi but me pasa di*

I know they would have shaped beautifully
cut words had they moved but they stood
still

*yo te ka di bon bagi but mey yo pa te sa vini po te
di*

only fluttering slightly when she exhaled

leve le ka mutou pale ke upca pale

there was so much noise and so few
words but i heard her

All Of The Life In My Little Black Body

la te ne telma dezod e pe pues pamol, but mey tan ne

I heard her

mey tan ne

I need water, love, sun, wind, strong hands, soft eyes, lines, bridges, songs and I need to be held and let go and i need that repeated

me duswe dlo, la mete, gaso mwe, va, force a la meng, mol zeu, aling, a po, sahte, mu bozey chebe, mu bozey la jey, mu vele ey way pete

I heard her

mey tan ne

I got up and walked out of the room and while I didn't bother to speak I know she heard me say I'd be back in a familiar tongue

me le vay, ek me soti ah shamla, me pa te pale but me tan yu, me ke vewey

*Creole (patios/patwa) spoken by Monica Holder in Anse La Raye, St. Lucia; learned beginning in 1971.

Austin Vandorian Grier

Sympathy For The Devil

I owe you an apology for my apology; it will not be one of those hearty offerings furnished out of based remorse or obstinate sorrow, it will not be an apology at all. I know I am beyond that. I still believe in penitence but there is a disquieting banality that escorts apologies so I am beyond forgiving because I cannot insult you anymore. I have to do right by you, which means I cannot apologize. It would be misguided and deceitful to say that I am sorry when I really mean to say that I am a man. I have gone over this in my head countless times; being remorseful and being a black man are beginning to sound synonymous. I waited this long because I wanted you to be able to believe that I know that there is no chance in hell that you could look past my trespasses. I am not seeking your forgiveness. I just wanted to be able to share the truth with you while you were capable of believing that there wasn't an ulterior motive.

I am a weapon. I was made this way. Though my intention is not to placate you by leading you to believe that I am incapable of salvaging some degree of agency for myself, I would have you know that such notions do not come easy. Men born like me must excavate themselves to find identity after suffering anodizing by assimilation and must risk cracking their skulls open while hammering their heads against their chests in pursuit of a truer self. Everything that was not taken from me was used as a justification to kill me and all I got in return was the reality that I am not my own. I am an instrument. I was made this way.

There is a kind of wretched, searing sobriety that is requisite when crafting men like me in a country like the one I have lived in for all of these years. I know that I am a valuable brew that a sober man prepared with the intention of consuming until his intoxication overcame him. I know that men as deliberate as surgeons cut me from myself; I know they employed Kevorkian mercy so that I could die in peace ignorant to precepts of abundance.

And then we got free. We didn't have to wait in the barn to be butchered and abused anymore, now we were free range and we could wander around and witness a world we could not enjoy before being cut to pieces and gobbled. For men like me captivity and freedom are equally traumatizing. There is no shelter and no way to protect my head from the blows. Being alive and black and a man is a blow. Nothing can protect you from that. They come swiftly too, strikes to the soul that lacerate and redact the spirit leaving men with torn sails amidst an anemic gale. I have been out at sea and out of my mind, reduced and pushed into a corner. My children were taken, as was my wife, my education, my plight, my love, my penis and my faculties. When I was finally stripped of it all I was mocked and called as animal; they hurled their insults at me and while I endured tornadoes of confliction and rage it hailed down on my head.

I raged and my hatred gave me a fever that boiled my blood until it turned to oil and I became a loveless bomb. And then I imploded.

I met you when I was picking up the pieces. I am sure that I looked certain of myself but I was not. I had no clue who I was and how could I have known? What does it even mean to be me? What history could I reference? There's no family crest for me. There's no identity for me. I had to create myself but I am mortal and lacking in foresight and discernment. So I recreated myself in the image of the only maker I could identify. I made myself a ravager. I made myself a solider. I made myself a conqueror.

I conquered you like I had conquered so many before you because you were my identity. There was no me without you, without what I thought I was. You were my food and I consumed you like I had been consumed. After I had swallowed you whole you became like me, tainted and angry, distrusting, isolated and ambitious. I cannot ask you to forgive me for that. I became familiar with my method and called it love and came to recognize it's effects and normalized them. I became so repugnant at one point that I approached all intimacy with incredulousness and regarded any love that did not leave wraiths in its wake as tenuous.

And then I came to myself. I imagine this is the duality the elder spoke of. Perhaps he meant it in a more philosophical way but I felt as if I had just been revived and made aware of what I had done as Mr. Hyde. All of the pain and destruction that was in front of me was overwhelming and then there was the manhunt. They were still after me. I ran. I ran from you and from them, my purpose, my gifts, my legacy, my opportunity and myself. I ran away and I was gone for a long time.

I'm back now. The first thing I did was come here to tell you where I have been and what I found out. I know that what I am going to tell you has been knowledge you have harbored all along but I had to go see for myself. I had to know.

I found myself out there drifting in a sea of violence and lust. I was dazed and confused, bloodthirsty and unaware of how to get home. I jumped onto my ship and came face to face with myself and I told him these things.

We have suffered a great deal but we are greater than the sum of the crimes committed against us. We are love. We are pride. We are strength. We are history. We are legacy. We have a woman and a purpose to return to. We have a village to build and children to raise up. We do not have to be angry because our joy is frightening enough. We do not have to beg for what we can build ourselves. We can go home.

And then I asked him to do the same thing I am going to ask of you. Do not waste your forgiveness on me because you have suffered enough at my hand but forgive those who have trespassed against me, scaring and wounding me. Forgive them for catapulting me into insanity. Forgive them for setting the table on my back and denying me food. Forgive them for believing themselves to be greater than we, for they have erred and are mistaken.

Please do not argue with me, my intention is to get you into Heaven, forgive them, love thy neighbor as thy self and have sympathy for the Devil.

All Of The Life In My Little Black Body

www.ingramcontent.com/pod-product-compliance
Lightning Source LLC
Chambersburg PA
CBHW030005110426
42736CB00040BA/514

9780578165714